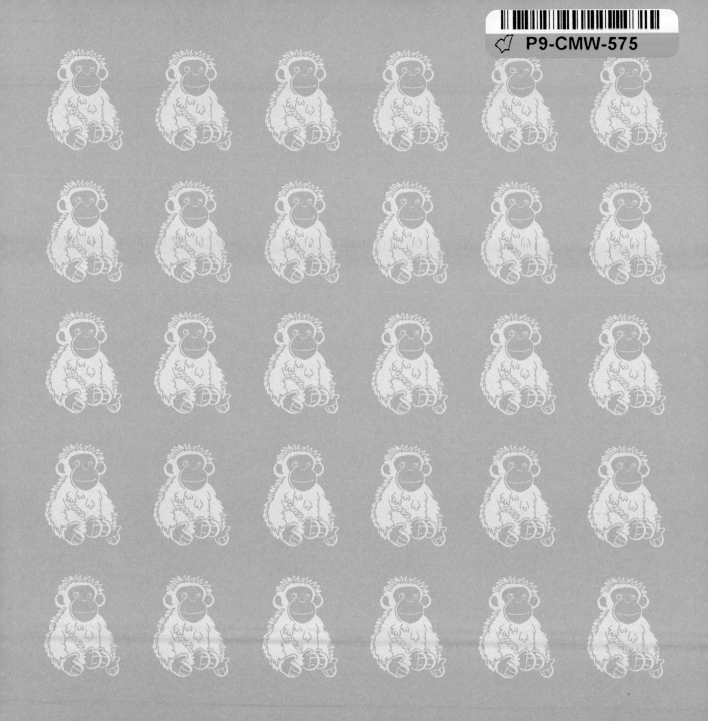

ORDINARY
PEOPLE
CHANGE
the
WORLD

I am
Jane Goodall

10-9-17
Happy Birthday
Lailana
Love
Howdy

BRAD MELTZER
illustrated by Christopher Eliopoulos

DIAL BOOKS FOR YOUNG READERS

I am **Jane Goodall.**

On my first birthday, my father bought me a cuddly toy chimpanzee named Jubilee.

I loved Jubilee.
I mean it.
Loved.

I used to carry Jubilee with me *everywhere*.
As I got older, when I'd line up all my toys and play teacher,
Jubilee was the one who had his own chair.

At five years old, I was curious to learn how chickens lay eggs, so I crawled into my grandmother's henhouse to watch.

At first, all the hens were scared of me.

Then I decided to crouch in the corner. If I had moved, the hens would've run away. I was patient, though.

Finally, after all the hours of waiting, I saw what I was looking for. The hen gave a little wiggle and . . .

Plop!
There was an egg.

WHERE WERE YOU?

YOU'VE BEEN MISSING FOR SO LONG WE SENT OUT A SEARCH PARTY!

YOU'LL NEVER BELIEVE WHERE EGGS COME FROM!

It was my first research project.

In addition to animals, I also loved nature.
I named the chestnut tree Nooky, and the beech tree Beech.
Beech was my favorite.

THANK YOU, BEECH, FOR LETTING ME READ UP HERE.

Oh, that was another
thing I loved: Reading.

Back then, my family didn't have a lot of money.
To get books, we went to the library.
When I was seven years old, I got a book that would change my life.

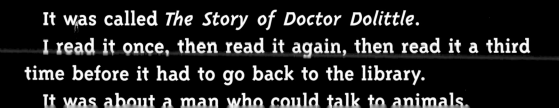

It was called *The Story of Doctor Dolittle*.
I read it once, then read it again, then read it a third time before it had to go back to the library.
It was about a man who could talk to animals.

In the book, there's a parrot who says that if you want to learn how animals talk, you need the "power of observation."

But what I remember most is the part where Dr. Dolittle and his animal friends are being chased and they come to a cliff.

HOW ARE WE EVER GOING TO GET ACROSS?

Right there, the monkeys joined hands and feet. They *became* the bridge.

Isn't that beautiful?

We can accomplish anything by working together.

After reading that book, I vowed that I would go to Africa and live among the animals.

By the time I was twelve, I had my own nature group: the Alligator Club.

My friends and I raised money to help old horses, we took nature walks, and wrote down what we saw (or at least I did).

And if you wanted to have a high rank in the club...

Was I the best student?
Not really.
On school days, it was hard for me to wake up.
I didn't like being indoors.
But if we were outside, or there were animals around—
that's when I'd get excited.

I wanted a job where I could learn more about animals.
But back then, if you were a girl, people didn't think you could become a scientist.
They expected girls to become nurses, secretaries, or teachers.

I wanted to go to Africa.
I wanted to study animals.
Luckily, my mom always told me:

IF YOU REALLY WANT SOMETHING, WORK HARD FOR IT.

IF YOU DON'T GIVE UP, YOU'LL FIND A WAY.

I never forgot that.

Soon, I had my chance.

One of my school friends invited me to visit her family in Kenya.

To pay for the trip, I worked as a waitress and hid my money under the carpet.

One day, I closed the curtains, counted it all, and...

The trip took twenty-one days by boat.

I was twenty-three years old.

It all seemed like a dream, until I saw a giraffe, who stared directly at me.

It had dark eyes, long lashes, a black tongue, and was chewing acacia thorns.

I knew my dream was coming alive.
Finally, I was in the Africa of Dr. Dolittle.

Two months later, my life changed again.
Someone told me: "If you are interested in animals, you must meet..."

Dr. Leakey was an anthropologist, which means he studied how humans live, and also a paleontologist, which means he studied fossils and bones.

At first, he hired me as a secretary.

But he was quickly impressed with what I knew about animals, including his own pets.

Eventually, Dr. Leakey told me about a new job studying chimpanzees up close.

He said going into the forest would be hard.

It would be dangerous.

But if we could find out how chimps live today, we'd learn more about how our own prehistoric ancestors used to live.

For a year, I read everything I could about chimpanzees.

I was also told that women couldn't be alone in the forest.

They said I needed a guide, plus a companion.

My mum offered to come.

I was ready.

I'll never forget the day: July 16, 1960—the day I first set foot in what is today Gombe National Park in Tanzania, Africa. At twenty-six years old, I had finally made it to the home of chimpanzees.

It was a place that would change my life.

During one of my first explorations, we saw two chimpanzees eating in a tall tree.

They noticed us and ran away.

THEY'RE SCARED OF US.

The next day, we didn't see any chimps.

There were no chimps the day after that either.

For months, I'd try to get close, but they kept running away.

Then I started going alone.

Just me.

I'd go to a high area called the Peak and look down with my binoculars.

In time, I saw that the chimpanzees would hang out in groups of six or fewer.

The female chimps would be with the children. The male chimps would be with one another.

These weren't mindless animals. This was a community.

Still, it took nearly a *year* before I could get within one hundred yards of the chimpanzees.

One day, I came back to camp and found out:

ONE OF THE MALE CHIMPANZEES TOOK OUR FOOD, INCLUDING YOUR BANANAS.

FANTASTIC!

THAT MEANS THEY'RE NOT SCARED OF ME NOW.

I BET HE'LL BE BACK TOMORROW.

The next day, I waited.
And waited.
There were no chimpanzees in sight.

Then, at four p.m., I heard a rustling noise by my tent.

It was the large male chimpanzee with a thick beard.

DAVID GREYBEARD.

That was the name I gave him.

Back then, people told me there was a "certain way" to study animals—that I shouldn't give the chimpanzees names.

They said animals were supposed to have numbers, not names.

Why?

They thought animals didn't have personalities or emotions.

They thought that if we gave them names, we'd start pretending they were like us.

But that's what no one realized.
They *were* like us.
That day, David Greybeard took
my nuts. And my bananas.

A month later,
he took one from
my hand!

Even later, out in the forest, he slowly approached me
and checked to see if I had a banana in my pocket.
It was one of my proudest moments: having the other
chimpanzees now understand that I wasn't a threat.

Over time, by seeing the chimpanzees as individuals,
I could truly understand them.

David was calm, though he
liked getting what he wanted.

Goliath was easily excited.

William was shy.

Old Flo was a strong mother, always
bringing her daughter and son.

As I watched, I learned one of the coolest things of all.
One day, I saw David Greybeard stripping leaves from a twig,
then sticking the twig into a termite mound.

He wasn't just using the twig as a tool.
He had *made* that tool.

Before that, scientists thought only humans could make tools.
There was no doubt now that these animals were intelligent.

Every night, I'd write in my journal about what I observed. And every day, I saw the chimpanzees doing the same things we do:

Holding hands.

Tickling.

Kissing.

Even patting backs to reassure each other.

The more I observed, the more I learned.

Soon, I had so much information, I needed a tape recorder.

Then, I needed an assistant to help observe all the other chimpanzee families in the forest.

Six years later, what started with a notepad and binoculars became a full research center.

Now *I* was the one in charge.

ISN'T IT WONDERFUL?

LOOK WHAT WE CAN BUILD TOGETHER!

Today, thanks to our work in Tanzania, the whole world knows that animals have their own personalities and complex relationships.

In my life, people told me there was
a "certain way" to do things:
a "certain way" to study animals,
a "certain way" that girls should behave.
They told me to follow the rules.
Instead, I followed my gut.

In your life, it will be easy to see how others are "different" from you.

But there's so much more to gain if you instead see how *alike* we all are.

All of us—all living things—share so much.

We have so many things in common.

When we realize that and look out for each other . . .

I am Jane Goodall,
and I see so much that we
have in common.

Watch. Observe. Be patient.
It'll teach you this:
We don't own this Earth.
We share it.

Listen to the feelings in your heart.
We are responsible for the animals around us.
We must take care of them.
When one of us is in trouble—be it human,
creature, or nature itself—we must reach out
and help.
When we do, we build a bridge...

a bridge that will
carry all of us.

"You cannot get through a single day without having an impact on the world around you. What you do makes a difference, and you have to decide what kind of difference you want to make." —Jane Goodall

Timeline

APRIL 3, 1934	NOVEMBER 1941	1957	JULY 16, 1960	NOVEMBER 4, 1960
Born in London, England	Reads *The Story of Doctor Dolittle* by Hugh Lofting	First visit to Africa; meets Louis Leakey	First day in Gombe National Park, Tanzania	Observes David Greybeard using a twig as a tool

Jane as a
toddler with
Jubilee

Jane with
David
Greybeard,
early 1960s

Jane with Dr.
Leakey

Jane with
Roots & Shoots members

1966

Receives PhD in
ethology, Cambridge
University

1967

Jane's son, Hugo
(nicknamed "Grub"),
is born

1967

Publishes book
*My Friends the Wild
Chimpanzees*

1977

Founds the Jane
Goodall Institute

1991

First meeting that
inspires Roots &
Shoots

TODAY

Jane is still alive and working
to protect chimpanzees and
our environment

For Lila and Teddy, who taught me
how much animals should be loved.

And for Amy Waggs & Kim Chi, for the same.
—B.M.

For Buddy Scalera, who always makes time
to listen to my problems and gives to others
without expecting in return. A true friend.
—C.E.

For historical accuracy, we used Dr. Goodall's actual dialogue whenever possible. For more of Dr. Goodall's true voice, we recommend and acknowledge *My Life with the Chimpanzees* and *In the Shadow of Man* by Jane Goodall.

Special thanks to Dr. Jane Goodall and all our friends at the Jane Goodall Institute.

SOURCES

My Life with the Chimpanzees by Jane Goodall (Simon & Schuster, 1996)
In the Shadow of Man by Jane Goodall (Mariner, 2010)
Jane Goodall: The Woman Who Redefined Man
by Dale Peterson (Mariner, 2008)
The Story of Doctor Dolittle by Hugh Lofting (Yearling, 1988)

FURTHER READING FOR KIDS

Me … Jane by Patrick McDonnell (Little, Brown, 2011)
The Watcher: Jane Goodall's Life with the Chimps by Jeannette
Winter (Schwartz & Wade, 2011)
Who Is Jane Goodall? by Roberta Edwards (Grosset & Dunlap, 2012)
Chimpanzee Children of Gombe by Jane Goodall (Minedition, 2014)

ABOUT THE JANE GOODALL INSTITUTE

Founded in 1977, the Jane Goodall Institute continues Dr. Goodall's pioneering research on chimpanzee behavior—research that transformed scientific perceptions of the relationship between humans and animals. Today, the Institute is a global leader in the effort to protect chimpanzees and their habitats. It also is widely recognized for establishing innovative community-centered conservation and development programs in Africa, and Jane Goodall's Roots & Shoots, the global environmental and humanitarian youth program, which has groups in more than 120 countries. For more information please visit www.janegoodall.org.

ABOUT JANE GOODALL'S ROOTS & SHOOTS

Founded in 1991 by Dr. Jane Goodall and a group of Tanzanian students, the Roots & Shoots program is about making positive change happen—for communities, for animals and for the environment. With more than 150,000 groups of young people in 130+ countries, the Roots & Shoots network connects youth of all ages who share a desire to create a better world. Young people identify problems in their communities and take action. Through service projects, youth-led campaigns and an interactive website, Roots & Shoots members are making a difference across the globe. For more information, please visit www.rootsandshoots.org.

DIAL BOOKS FOR YOUNG READERS • Penguin Young Readers Group • An imprint of Penguin Random House LLC • 375 Hudson Street, New York, NY 10014

Text copyright © 2016 by Forty-four Steps, Inc. • Illustrations copyright © 2016 by Christopher Eliopoulos.

Library of Congress Cataloging-in-Publication Data
Names: Meltzer, Brad, author. • Eliopoulos, Christopher, illustrator. • Title: I am Jane Goodall / Brad Meltzer ; illustrated by Christopher Eliopoulos.
Description: New York, NY : Dial Books for Young Readers, 2016. • Series: Ordinary people change the world • Audience: Ages 5 to 8. • Includes bibliographical references.
Identifiers: LCCN 2015044312 • ISBN 9780525428497 (hardcover) • Subjects: LCSH: Goodall, Jane, date—Juvenile literature. • Primatologists—England—Biography—Juvenile literature.
Chimpanzees—Tanzania—Gombe Stream National Park—Juvenile literature. • Classification: LCC QL31.G58 M45 2016 • DDC 599.8092—dc23 LC record available at http://lccn.loc.gov/2015044312

Photos on pages 38–39 © the Jane Goodall Institute

Printed in China • 10 9 8 7 6 5 4 3 2 1
Designed by Jason Henry • Text set in Triplex • The artwork for this book was created digitally.

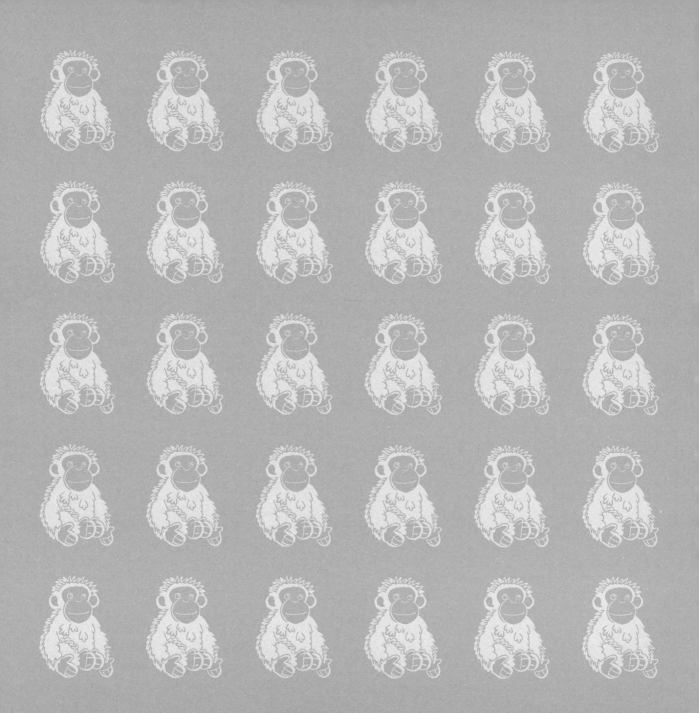